Poets' Choice

Dianne C. Braley

THE HEROIN ADDICT'S WIFE

Poems From A Past Long Buried

Edited By Tasneem

Published By

Poets' Choice®

Poets Choice and Free Spirit LLC
1216 Broadway Floor 2 PMB 1010 - New York NY 10001 - USA

www.poetschoice.in
Phone: +1 914-650-2747 (Primary) + 1 646 974 9406 (Fax)

1st Edition November 2025

Edited By Tasneem

Printed In India

ISBN: 978-93-6617-793-9
BCID: 355-17710229

Visit www.bookcrossing.com

Instagram - *@freespiritpublisher*
Youtube - *@freespiritpublisher*

Table of Contents

SICK

Two hours—

but I'd drive anywhere

to get my fix.

There, on the corner

beneath a grimy street sign—

there it is.

And I pull over

for the drug deal,

the transaction I return to

over and over again.

Because I do.

Because I'm sick.
Not a needle in my vein,
but a magnet to my blood.
You blink, seeing me.
You swagger, being you.
It's you with the tracks.
It's you, strung out—again.
And I'm here,
our baby in tow—
the creation of love,
the creation of lies—
picking up you
because you never can.
The heat hisses off the sidewalk
when you get in,
and it ignites the space between us.
It always fucking does.
That's why I return.
And return.
And return.
I burn.

And I hate myself for it—
the kiss,
the pull,
the fucking draw
that shouldn't be.
You love venom.
And I love you
because I never knew
when I fell—
but didn't I?
With red flags on fire.
But red flags feel safe.
I've been blanketed in them
since a girl.
My father.
Now you.
I am home in hell.
You speak without words.
Empty promises.
You don't have to.
I'm still here—

lovesick,

strung-out

on fucking you.

THIS ISLAND

Got a smoke? Of course—you always do,
You pass it slow beneath the Vineyard sky.
September salt clings thick like morning dew,
Our fingers brush, the tide begins to rise.
The dock still sways with echoes of last night,
The lighthouse blinking warnings I ignore.
I fall from grace, from pedestal to plight,
Into your arms, the storm I once adored.
The cottage breathes with sun and cigarettes,
The radio plays our war-torn lullabies.
Each kiss a curse I never will forget,

Each breath a lie I'm far too dazed to fight.

So let it burn—this island, us, the bed.

The Vineyard holds our ghosts and all we've said.

PRETENDERS

Nothing's right—
but it could be.
It was.
Wasn't it?
Or was it a dream,
stitched from salt and need,
a house I built from smoke,
a mirror I begged to lie—
you were who I made you.
Pretend. Pretend.
We are the pretenders.

Your skin sweats bullets.

Your eyes roll back

like tides retreating

from a wreck they've seen before.

Slap.

"What's wrong?"

Time gallops

when I need it to crawl.

Pretend. Pretend.

We are the pretenders.

"We're going to be late."

The party.

My jewelry—

vanished like your promises.

Something's wrong.

You nod like a marionette

cut loose mid-performance.

The floor drinks you in.

Pretend. Pretend.

We are the pretenders.

"Get up. We have to go."

The tracks.

Another slap.

A needle. A spoon.

Your body a cathedral to ruin.

Pretend. Pretend.

We are the pretenders.

Blinded by lust—

no, the echo of it.

I mistook the hunger for love,

the crash for the climb.

The ocean spit back your lies,

salt-licked and shining.

Pretend. Pretend.

We are the pretenders.

Get up.

We have a party.

BLACK HOLES

There's nothing there—

Not even lies in your eyes anymore.

Hollow. Wind-stripped.

Gone to sea like everything else we tried to bury.

Back to the slum streets we clawed out of—

the ones we swore we left behind.

But we didn't.

We dragged the dirt with us.

Smeared it across beauty.

Left venom in the sheets.

Fury in the walls.

Bruises where love was supposed to be.

You—

Perfect face, soft lips,

whispers like prayers by the ocean.

And I believed every one.

I wanted them true.

I chased the dream.

Again. Again.

But the veil lifted.

And now you rage because I *see.*

The secrets. The rot. The ruin.

All of it.

All of *you.*

There's nothing left to believe in.

I've become my mother.

You—my father.

No different.

Just children of cracked sidewalks and corner stores

that sell poison behind smiles.

We are the grime.

The stench in the stairwells.

The noise that never stops.

We are the streets.

We are filth.

But still,

I believe.

I’m not done.

HER

I want to know.

Not out of curiosity—

but torment.

What does *she* give you

that I never could?

That rush in your blood,

that hush behind your eyes,

when you sink into her.

It must be better than me.

Better than love.

Better than skin and breath and sweat

and the way I begged you to stay.

It must be.

Because you keep going back.

Her.

That's what I call it.

Her.

Because it's not a habit—

it's a *lover.*

It's a *whore.*

And you worship her.

She takes you whole,

and you offer yourself like prayer.

Again.

Again.

Your eyes flutter shut.

Your jaw unclenches.

The world vanishes.

We vanish.

You say you hate her,

but you always find your way to her door.

I see it—

you trying not to look.
But your veins look for her
before your mind does.
And I imagine her.
If she had a face—
that poison you crave—
I see her.
Long dark hair
and a mouth made for lies.
Breasts you'd sell me for.
Lips red enough to mark your soul.
A siren in a spike.
A goddess made of rot.
The seduction that kills you
slow.
And I wonder.
What does it feel like,
to give up everything
for a kiss from death?
I'll never know.
Not now.

Not with this pulse

growing inside me.

Our child.

Our maybe-redemption.

Our maybe-nothing.

Maybe you'll love him more than her.

Maybe this time,

we'll be enough.

But I know better.

You can't unlove her.

You can't unneed her.

Still, I wait.

Still, I bleed.

Still, I *hope.*

Because that's what fools do.

And I am the queen of them all.

THE COTTAGE BY THE SEA

In the cottage by the sea, I thought I knew,
Where stars once whispered what was meant to be,
But truth crept in, quiet and cruel, and true.
We moved like waves—your touch, the pull of you,
The air was thick with want and memory
In the cottage by the sea. I thought I knew.
Our bodies burned in passion, fierce and new,
While lies lay waiting, predictable like the tide—
But truth crept in, quiet and cruel, and true.
I saw the cracks beneath the calmest blue,
Still let you in, surrendered willingly,

In the cottage by the sea. I thought I knew.
You smiled, you smoked, the silence split us through—
And I stayed put, heart dumb with loyalty,
Though truth crept in, quiet and cruel, and true.
And if I could go back, I'd still choose you—
The stars, the scars, the salt, the memory.
In the cottage by the sea, I thought I knew,
But truth crept in, quiet and cruel, and true.

OFF-SEASON VOWS

Off-season winds and silence
wrap around us beneath the gazebo.
A dusting of snow softens the street,
Christmas lights blink,
faint and unsure.
The lighthouse wreath glows
down the crooked path to the shore.
Chappy waits in the distance.
So do we—
for you. Again.
We just said *I do.*

The cake waits, untouched.

Let's go inside and see.

But you're not there.

You never are.

Gone—

like before,

when you vanished at your mother's,

or after work,

or into thin air.

A ghost again,

on the biggest day,

the best day—

the day it was supposed to be.

You left us,

your ship of fools.

And I—I knew.

Even as I walked to meet you,

steps slow, dress dragging,

I felt the wrongness,

coiled and quiet.

This union…

I didn't know why.

But I knew.

Oh, what a fool I was.

How could I not see?

I did.

I just didn't want to.

Because you smell,

feel,

taste

like sin dressed in silk.

And you lie like you breathe.

And I swallow it whole.

We're here now.

The horizon still pretends.

Isn't this what we do?

We say *I do*.

But I didn't have to.

I chose it—

because you smell,

feel,

taste

like something I'd follow anywhere.

No need to vanish.

You reappear,

all better.

All fixed.

Everything's fine.

Let's cut the cake.

Or maybe

our wrists.

GONE

My lungs empty
into a house
that isn't.
It feels.
It thinks.
Without you.
Love explodes.
Then it all does—
us, life,
this fucking world.
A hell bubble.

Blue lights fade.

Relief.

They take you.

Far.

No way back.

No way to me.

Always,

you find me.

Weak.

You seep in.

Everywhere.

I thought it was passion.

Once.

But I've been wrong before.

Love hurts—

that's normal,

right?

You'd say so.

You'd say I don't love

because I leave.

Because I made you.

I sink.

Swim.

Sink again.

Down.

Down.

Down.

Drown

if I stay.

Sometimes,

it feels easier

to stop

than to run.

I've tried before.

But I stayed.

Too long.

Lost me

in you.

Your sickness.

Your lies.

Your sour soul.

Gone.

Far.

Now you're caged.

Blue lights gone.

Bars between us.

Will I see you?

Will you find me?

Save me.

THE TIDE

Who are you?
A fool.
I wasn't looking,
but you came anyway—
persistent,
cocky,
sure.
Of me?
Of yourself?
Of something
I couldn't see.
I had tides to chase,
winds to follow,

bigger things
than you.
But you kept coming—
like the sea
on a rising moon,
relentless,
pulling.
And there I was,
on the porch,
cottage door open,
salt on my lips,
waves at my back.
Still no.
Not me.
Not yet.
But maybe—
just a little—
a fling by the shore,
something fleeting,
like sand slipping
through fingers.
Then you leaned me back—
a kiss,
all energy,

smooth and fire,
crashing,
like surf on rocks.
And suddenly,
I belonged to the tide—
no longer free,
only pulled.

CONFIDENCE IN TRACK PANTS

The metal doors slam shut behind you,
and you wave goodbye to your captors
like they're old friends.
You give them purpose—
them, and the state of Massachusetts.
Where are you going
with your cigarettes
and that forty-dollar deposit
you flipped into hundreds?
Hustling.

Always hustling.
Even when the poison's gone,
even when the party's over,
you can't escape the game.
Always wheeling, always dealing,
no matter what your family feels.
No matter what.
But here you are,
free again,
swaggering in those track pants—
confidence stitched into cheap polyester.
A reminder of my youth.
And I'm here,
waiting outside those gates,
hating myself for it,
longing for your touch.
Hating and wanting.
Hating and wanting.
Until I'm hollow.
You stroll by, unfazed,
like this is just another day.

And to me, it stinks—
it gnaws,
it twists my insides raw.
But still I wait,
craving the brush of your hands
just so I can hate us again.
I hate you.
I hate me more.
Next year, we'll be back here,
false confidence in track pants,
me needing a scrub
to scrape you out of my life.
Maybe next time
I'll be closer.
Maybe someday
this will just be a memory—
a scar
that ruined me
for anyone else.
Maybe someday.

THE RETURNING

I prepare myself for when you're finally done,
My words sharpened, trained to cut you through.
Three days have passed, and still you haven't come.
I toss your black garbage bag, ripped open and raw.
My words sharpened, trained to cut you through.
I locked the door, but you know how to get in.
I toss your black garbage bag, ripped open and raw.
A wave of heat, my ears ring loud with sin.
I locked the door, but you know how to get in.
The wind knocks once—I hold my breath, afraid.
A wave of heat, my ears ring loud with sin.
I call again—no answer, nothing said.
The wind knocks once—I hold my breath, afraid.

Maybe you're gone, strung out and in the street.
I call again—no answer, nothing said.
I dream of you collapsed beneath my feet.
Maybe you're gone, strung out and in the street.
Three days have passed, and still you haven't come.
I dream of you collapsed beneath my feet.
I prepare myself for when you're finally done.

BUT LOVE

You offered nothing
but love—
and that was enough.
Like the moon is enough for the tide,
the tide for the shore,
the shore for the people—
your love was enough for me.
Until it wasn't.
Until it drowned us.
The moon fell from the sky,
the tide swallowed the beaches,

the people fled,

and we were gone—

you and me.

SPIRITS

Head in hands,
elbows on the table—
a coffee mug
with no coffee.
Mornings were for spirits.
Afternoons too.
Evenings, especially.
Good times don't last.
Spirits break,
and so do
others.

Still, he sat—
morning
after
morning,
drinking
to forget,
to feel,
to vanish,
to exist.
And I—
I was one of the others.
I watched.
Lived in the wreckage.
Forgotten.
Now,
I teach myself
to forget.
Because
I
love
you.

How can that be?

Didn't

I

see?

SECRETS

Secrets seep,
slip through seams,
slide from the shadows you swore were sealed.
Locks loosen,
latches lift,
keys kiss daylight from the dirt.
Who were you hiding from?
Me?
No.
No. No. No.
You were hiding from you—

your loathing,

your lurking,

your glass-shard gaze.

Mirror smashed,

mouth spitting venom at your own skin.

I saw the sin.

I saw the truth.

Now it's stitched to me,

threaded in my veins,

beating where my blood should be.

It was never buried deep.

It bled in the heat of our sweat,

flared in the fire of our eyes,

fell in the flood of our tears.

It lurked in theft,

in threat,

in the thrum of fear.

Now I hold a secret too—

one I'll swallow whole,

let it rot in my ribs where no light lives.

I'll bolt your demon in a box,

swallow the key,
sink the lock to the bottom of me.
If you'll let me,
we'll break his bones to splinters,
beat him until even his shadow surrenders,
and the ash of him—
we'll hide it in the hollow.
But I can't stay.
And they know.
I knew better—
didn't I?
No.
Now I'm draped in your dirt,
diseased with your dust.
I was clean once—
pure as a pulse—
but your grime grips me,
and I wish—
God, I wish—
it was only a dream.

AGAIN

Breath.

Shudder.

Again.

Your arms—closing in.

Again.

Salt slicks my lips.

Earth hums on your skin.

The tang of you—

thick in my mouth.

Again.

The air swells.

Hot.

Heavy.

It clings,

coats my lungs in sweat.

The spin begins—

a slow tilt,

a pull into something

too deep to fight.

Love burns,

crawls beneath my skin.

Hate chills,

cuts like glass in my veins.

Here—

gone.

Gone—

here.

Lost.

Found.

Your heartbeat pounds in my ear.

Mine stumbles to keep time.

It can't go on.

(It can't.)

It can't go on.

(It does.)

I'M STILL HERE

I'm on my knees, pulling the last petal, the only pink left from spring,

and I'm thinking how I fell, how I keep falling—

so in love I slipped straight into hell,

calling for help in a voice I don't even recognize,

a cry that doesn't carry, a scream that's swallowed before it leaves my mouth.

I want out of this scene, this scorched garden where roses burned in June,

and I stood there watching them blacken, knowing I couldn't save them—

and after all the rain, after all the trying, I couldn't save myself either.

I thought I could, but pain is a patient thing; it waits,

and when it moves in, it rearranges everything you are.

And I wonder if there's anything left of me worth keeping.

If I go, what if he goes too, what if he disappears entirely—

dies like the roses,

dies like the part of me that used to believe in anything good.

So I scream, loud enough to shatter the stillness,

and this time I know the sound is mine.

I'm here.

I'm still here.

And then the roses return, soft and shameless,

as if they never burned at all.

It's spring again,

and they are pink.

NO MATTER

Danger signs glow like lanterns,
and I walk toward the light.
Isn't that the truth—
that love ignores the warning?
Your skeletons rattle in the dark,
but I cradle them as my own.
Your love is a worn coat,
familiar in its fraying seams,
and familiar feels safe.
My darling, you are a mirror,
reflecting every place I've fled.

In sickness, in health,
until death pulls the curtain,
I cannot run from myself.
So I give you my heart—
and we dance,
and we burn,
and you are my drug.
But I am not yours.
Your eyes turn to her
as if she is the only star,
and I am only the dark.
I can't match her pull,
no matter how I ache,
no matter how I bleed,
no matter how I try.

AND AGAIN

Bombs gift-wrapped in love letters
I pull at the beautiful bow,
and January spills me open
on the edge of new snow.
Ah, but the bombs—
they keep me breathing,
because survival has its own kind of glory.
I set sail on promises
that snap like twigs in a winter forest,
breaking under the weight of your lips.
They fall,

sink into the dirt,
and drift away in dust.
Ashes to ashes.
Dust to dust.
How can something so alive
die so completely?
Like us.
Like snow, fresh-fallen.
I only know the heat that lingers
when a promise is kept—
even a piece of one,
a speck.
But they always fall.
Down to the ground.
Again.
And again.
And again.

I WALK

I walk the dirt roads of East Chop,
past summer homes sealed tight,
their windows clouded with salt from storms long gone.
The air is sharp with sea and pine,
the kind of air that once made me breathe deeper.
Now it only stings.
Once, walking here was pleasure—
waves folding against the rocks,
gulls cutting across the sky,
the rhythm of our laughter keeping pace with my steps.
Now the ocean sounds like goodbye.

My legs are lead,
each step heavier than the last.
My heart—
God, my heart—
pulls me backward,
back to the rooms we filled and emptied,
to the bad as much as the good,
because even the bad was ours.
The ferry waits at the end of the road,
engines low and patient,
its decks yawning toward the open water.
It knows I'll board.
It always knew.
The sea between us will widen with every churn of its wake,
swallowing the shore,
blurring the line where your world touches mine.
I don't want to go.
I want to stay where my heart still beats—
rooted in your hands,
anchored in our tide.

But my legs know the truth.

They carry me toward the leaving I didn't choose.

So I go—

carrying only the shell of myself,

while the living part stays with you.

The ferry groans, the ropes are pulled,

and the ocean opens its mouth.

It takes me because it must.

I go because I must.

THE NIGHT

Resting eyes, a heavy womb—I listen.
Whispers in the dark from the other room—I hear.
I once trusted the night and its wisdom,
Still and black, with nothing to fear.
Rustling, rummaging, hushed tones,
A door, an engine—I dash.
I follow with aching bones,
Thumping, throbbing—a near crash.
Shadows stretch long in a lonely driveway,
Silhouettes meet for the exchange.
Dreams grow feet and run away,

And nothing, again, has changed.
Except I hide my purse now,
And hide my pain from view.
Your sickness you won't avow,
But to it, you are true.
I breathe, but I am dead.
You lie—you are dead too.
My body begs for bed,
And you are nothing I thought I knew.

THE UNRAVELING

Eyes of fire,
skin against skin—
love tangled with hate,
passion with rage,
a blaze that leaves
nothing standing.
The carousel groans,
melodies circling,
round and round,
like vows unraveling.
Warm blankets,

salted air,
sickness and health,
faith gone brittle.
Scorn is a crown,
jaded hearts rust,
breath grows shallow,
the body drifts—
a slap,
a jolt back.
Whispers of blame:
fuck you,
fuck me too.
We trade comebacks
for broken glass,
dreams that collapse
before they're named.
Hope still pines,
but nothing shifts.
The spoons and the needles
keep their vigil.
Infinity whispers forever,

but death waits patient,

its shadow in the doorway.

So we say goodbye,

then return with hello,

again and again—

one shot,

the world goes silent.

It's over.

(It never is.)

NEEDLE AND SPOON

The moon commands the tide,
and still it cannot move you.
Your body writhes,
my heart is a hollow shell,
emptied by every promise
that needles and spoons keep.
The sun rises too soon,
searing, merciless—
and you reach again
for the only mercy you know.
Death whispers soft,

but you answer louder.
Waves crash along the dunes,
salt baptizes us clean.
For a fleeting breath,
we believe in freedom,
we believe in rebirth.
An osprey circles and cries—
we lift our heads,
but sight is gone.
Needle and spoon—
they wait in the dark,
patient gods of hunger,
their orders obeyed:
cook, draw, fill.
The tide comes in,
the tide goes out.
And we are carried,
again and again,
by needle and spoon.

PLEASE HELP

Brave—I'm here, breaking open,
asking for help. Please help. Please.
Sever the chain, sever my limbs,
so they cannot hold on to him,
to the saving, the fixing, the masochism
I've worn like a second skin.
Cut them—cut me down to bone.
Tell me I am fine, that I can survive this.
Because this has to end—
or it ends another way.
The circle turns, the cycle swells,

round and round the drain we go.
He's sinking, and I follow.
Down. Down. Down.
I can't pull him up—
I can't pull myself up.
Please help. Please.
Lend me your hands, your strength,
something to climb with,
something to run with,
to keep running, away, away.
Love spirals, love claws—
it scratches and bleeds me hollow.
I am clutching at nothing,
screaming at God,
pleading, *Please help. Please.*
It's been so long that I've only wilted,
a flower left too long in drought,
brown, brittle, dead at the edges,
but still with just enough lifeblood
to reach for him when he comes.
And he always comes.

I tell him to stay away.

I mean it.

I don't.

The truth thrashes between us—

I am done, or I am dead.

I wish I knew who wins.

He toys with poisons and fire,

and I play with him,

as though this dance were life itself.

Crying, screaming,

I unravel into the same refrain—

Please help. Please.

LAST RIDE

A year without you,

a month with someone new.

Skeletons unearthed, buried again,

the climb relentless, the hill unforgiving.

Love doesn't leave when you beg it to,

love lingers, heavy,

long after farewell.

I waved and turned,

diving into the pool of my own reflection.

Hello, stranger—

the one I had forgotten,

the one I had never truly met.

Now here you are.
And still, there you are,
waiting in the shadows,
searching for a crack,
a weakness,
a way back in.
I see you.
That day, that train.
One last ride, one last look.
Our child smiling in the back,
sunlight streaking across steel tracks
and the tracks on your arm.
I saw, and you knew I did.
You turned away.
No more denial.
No more pretending.
Only silence left to speak.
Take care of yourself, I said.
I reached for your arm,
you leaned in close.
Stop.
I pulled back.

The touch would unravel me,
my reflection swallowed whole by yours.
Your eyes wet,
your head bowed.
So tired.
"I can't do this anymore," you said.
"I know," I replied.
The train slowed,
the station neared.
One last meeting of eyes,
a half-smile,
an ending.
And then the birds sang into morning.
The call came,
the news followed.
You were gone.
And so was I.
But still, I live.
To die,
and to begin again.

Dear Reader,

We are ecstatic to note that you chose to read one of our publications. The time you invested into reading this book is much appreciated. We value your allegiance. As a give back present, we will be happy to share **'YOUR PICTURE HOLDING THIS BOOK'** on our *Official Social Media Handles* such as Facebook, Instagram and Twitter.

All you have to do is – send it to us.

1. Write Your Name

2. Review , if any

3. Subject Line of Email – Pic Holding Book (Book Name)

4. Image Attached – jpeg / gif/ png file.

Email it to – poetschoice@hotmail.com